D0841611

MINDFUL MONEY

A PATH TO SIMPLE FINANCES

MINDFUL MONEY

A PATH TO SIMPLE FINANCES

Linda Bessette

Bird Call Press

Little Rock, Arkansas

For ML

Thanks to everyone who read the manuscript
and suggested revisions.
I hope I have done your work justice.

Mindful Money
A path to simple finances

 Bird Call Press

© Copyright 2008 by Linda Bessette
Little Rock, Arkansas

All Rights Reserved.

Library of Congress Control Number: 2008931666

ISBN: 978-0-9791896-1-6

Book design, cover and typography by Patrick Houston
www.patrickhouston.com

This book was set in Caslon 224, a typeface derived from one originally cut
by the distinguished English letter-founder William Caslon (1692–1766)
and is known for its legibility and clarity.

Printed in the United States by Morris Publishing
3212 East Highway 30
Kearney, NE 68847
1-800-650-7888

CONTENTS

BE STILL

What does it mean to be mindful about your money? It means something very simple, but very specific. It means being completely awake to the present moment and to your relationship with money in that moment. You begin with the premise that every financial decision you make, no matter how big or how small, will have a consequence. It is your job to remind yourself of that. The consequence will occur whether you notice it or not. You may be moving so fast that you do not notice it, but that doesn't mean it did not occur. Each time you give yourself one minute, or thirty seconds, or even ten seconds, literally, to bring your awareness into the moment, to be fully present so that you can see the many facets of your interaction with money, you stay as fully connected to the reality of that moment as you can. When you are mindful, you are connected to each moment in a way that the 'fast life' does not allow.

This may seem like a strange way to begin a book about money, but in truth, many of you live as though you've been spun off from a wheel that was spinning so fast you couldn't hang on. You get thrown off at some point and while you are flying through the air, you pick up a mortgage here, a car payment there, and debt everywhere. You worry about the future while you ignore the present, and you live with a vague fear (or certainty) that you and your life are out of control. The problem is, you don't know how to regain control. You don't know how to stop flying through the air. And the worst of it is that even if you could figure out how to stop, you wouldn't know where to go or what to do next.

If you could find your way back to the wheel, the only safe place to stay would be in the center. As others fly off all around you, trying desperately to hang onto the spokes, the edges, the rims – the calm center is where you'd like to be. No stress, no pressure, just calm. You'd be tuned into your life, moment to moment.

Do you deserve peace of mind about your money? Of course you do. Does it require courage to admit that? Frequently. Many times your inability to handle your money in a way that brings you peace of mind is like a Zen koan. To answer the riddle you must stand still. If you run around and ask, why can't I make more money? Why don't I have more savings? Why do I have so much debt? Why can't I get ahead? Why can't I take a vacation? Then you will find there are no general answers to this endless litany of questions. The answer is singular to you and is revealed to you in the moment. If the moments are flying by at breakneck speed, you will miss them and all that they have to tell you. Instead of slowly discovering answers, you will rapidly drown in questions.

Can you buy things? Of course you can. If you live in the developed world nearly everything can be bought. That does not mean you can afford to buy these things, or that buying them is even a good idea for you, financially or otherwise. Do you deserve to have things? A new car? A vacation? Clothes? Of course, you deserve it. What human being is not deserving? Does deserving have anything to do with managing your money or making a financial plan? Not a thing.

Do you beat yourself up over past money decisions that you now judge to have been wrong? Do you obsess over these perceived mistakes? Whether the errors occurred forty minutes or forty years ago, they are all quite solidly in the past. You may look back and take what advice you can from those decisions, but that is all. You are in the present. You must remember that.

A big part of getting back to that calm center is to accept yourself wherever you are. In fact, this may be the most difficult part. To accept yourself is far more difficult than managing money. Money management is just simple math most of the time. But to meet yourself, perhaps for the first time, in a mindful moment, without judgment – this is big. It will let you awaken to the reality that you are not what you earn, where you live, what you do for a living, what your bank balance is, or what kind of car you drive. That realization can feel scary, then freeing, and then scary again. But you must have courage. You must meet the mindful you with complete acceptance. The mindful you is more vast than your circumstances. Your situation is not your life.

No one gets to live in this calm, free space all the time. But you can be vigilant, and you can remind yourself of it, moment to moment, even when you are struggling to pay the bills.

As you can probably tell, this book is meant for everyone. Age, gender, financial condition, or any other demographics are not deal-breakers here. Good money management –

money management that gives you peace of mind and helps you reach your goals – is appropriate for everyone. The size of your income makes no difference. Frequently, those with the most money manage it in the least efficient ways. An abundance of money can hide an abundance of mistakes.

So begin by being still. Have a seat. Get comfortable. Turn everything off. And breathe . . . maybe just three long breaths. Let's check in with reality. What is it? You have created your own life. No matter where you come from, what was given to you or taken away, how you were helped or hindered – the life you have *at this moment* is the result of every decision you have made up to this point. So assess your life. Are you pleased with it? Do you like what you have created? How much does your creation cost? Have you traded the precious time of your finite life for money in a way that makes you happy? Have you created a life that costs so much that you have sentenced yourself to working around the clock to earn the money to keep that life going? Do you work at a job you don't really enjoy or respect in order to obtain the money to buy yourself things that you feel will make you happy, better, more powerful, or more secure? Do you allow yourself to be treated badly in order to obtain money? Are you afraid to change your career because if you stopped being a whatever then you wouldn't know who you were?

Perhaps you are young and have not yet started your work life. Or maybe you are already retired from working. Maybe you have children. Perhaps they are still small and rely entirely upon you, or they are grown and lead their own lives. Your age does not matter. The stage of life you are in does not matter. Mindfulness works at all times.

If a person is forty years old and has saved five million dollars and wants to retire, most of you would think he could. However, if he has created a life that costs five hundred thousand dollars a year, then, simply put, he could only stop working for ten years before the five million would be gone. If he did not die at fifty years old, he would need to return to work.

So back to your life. Your creation. Are you balanced in your outlays of time and money, or are you out of balance? Are you totally stressed because of work, family, relationships, and money issues? Are you hanging onto the spoke of the wheel with just the tips of your fingers, fearing that you are going to go flying off into the cosmos at any moment? Do you currently take any steps to actually slow your life down and reduce stress or do you simply rush to the gym to walk on the treadmill or stop at the bar to relieve the stress that you have produced through your own decisions?

When you are mindful you slow down, you reflect for a moment, or perhaps for many moments; you assess the causes of your stress and you make genuine, good faith efforts to eliminate the activities causing those stresses. You learn to say no. It is not easy, but it is as necessary as air. Have you created an enormously expensive life that forces you to work constantly? Do you have emotional and psychological issues that keep you at a constant run in your head, or literally, in your life? Do you find that you never fully relax, never stop, never sleep deeply or for too long? Do you find yourself up in the middle of the night obsessing or ruminating over this or that?

The Buddhists have a funny saying: "Don't just do something, sit there". Most of you tend to do something even when you don't know what to do. You are as people standing on one side of a tennis court, wildly swinging your tennis racquet, sometimes one in each hand, except that no one has hit a ball to you. Being mindful is being present . . . aware . . . resting in the moment and ready for what comes next. When you employ mindfulness in your life, you become the hub of the wheel. You are no longer on the circumference, spinning out of control; you are the calm center.

When you employ mindfulness in handling your money and making your daily financial decisions, you become the calm center of your financial life. You are present and reflective, rather than running from here to there, swiping your credit cards without a thought, indebting yourself on a whim, investing in this or that, and signing contracts willy-nilly, all the while never allowing yourself to be fully aware of the consequences that your actions will produce. Because you do not notice the consequences, you think they do not exist. They do.

So, this book is called Mindful Money. I will ask you to slow down, perhaps just a bit at first and more as you become more comfortable in doing so. I will ask you to give yourself a moment of breathing room before each financial decision.

And I will remind you that this is a moment-to-moment process, not a one-time, screaming, careening event. If you make small changes, maybe even one a week, the rewards will be long lasting and you will take your life, your creation, in a new direction. The precious time you now spend worrying about money, obsessing over money, fearing money, or ignoring money will be freed up to be put to better use. You will begin to question things, regain the present, and gain control. The process is simple and it doesn't take much time. You don't need a computer, an iPod, financial software, a cell phone, or anything else electronic or expensive. The biggest thing you have to change is your mind.

BREATHE

Begin to think of your financial life in the form of concentric circles. In the smallest, innermost circle lie just the basics. Half of the world's population lives on less than two dollars a day. For those human beings, just surviving in the innermost circle is the work of every minute of every day of their lives. Obtaining food enough to eat, shelter from the cold, rain, and sun, and clothing for comfort and modesty become daily goals. The poor of the world win the game of life just by staying alive. Your life is so complicated by comparison. You must concern yourself with mortgages, IRAs, tuition bills, soccer practice, piano lessons, holiday and birthday presents, 401(k)s, and retirement. When you have lunch with your friends or colleagues and complain that you are broke, most of you only mean that you are temporarily low on funds. Some of you even feel that paying attention to money is crude, that money somehow cheapens what it touches. Thankfully, most of you do not have to live a life on less than two dollars a day.

So begin your practice of mindfulness by being grateful. And acknowledge your gratitude every day. You have decisions to make about money because you have money. You are fortunate to be in this predicament, and you should be grateful for it.

If you are able to cover the basics and you are fortunate enough to have money left over, then you find yourself naturally wanting to move to the next circle. This is where you begin to acquire assets: real property, savings, and non-necessities. You can purchase goods and services. You can own things. Perhaps a house, some furniture, some savings, probably a vehicle, and toys. Eventually you find that you need various types of insurance to protect those assets. You now occupy a place that many of your fellow human beings, even in the developed world, see only from a distance. You have moved beyond what you need just to survive, and you can turn your attention to things you might want.

After you've acquired assets, you might contemplate investing. This is the next circle – one that most of the world's population never sees. It is a rare place, indeed. Here is where you open your mind to a much more abstract concept: the notion that you can use your money for more than just staying alive or buying stuff. This is the level where you actually use your money to spin off more money. You invest some of your funds in the hope that your future will be secure financially or that you will have assets to leave to the next generation, thereby making their lives a little easier. Leaving anything of value to the next generation is a relatively new phenomenon, historically. While the super wealthy have always tended to take care of the next generation in an effort to hold onto political control, the bulk of the world's population generally has had nothing to hand down beyond the occasional keepsake, tool, trade or skill. Having the opportunity to consciously plan in this life to leave assets to the next generation is a privilege that has presented itself in history to only a few. And even though more people are now able to leave something to their children, the number of people doing so is still only a small fraction of the world's population.

Beyond this circle is a realm that I will simply call wealth. People with any amount of wealth frequently move large sums of money toward philanthropy. Charitable giving is done at all income levels but very large charitable gifts come only from a small percentage of the population and these frequently come from trusts or foundations that the wealthy have established.

Now, you might be thinking that the game is played by accumulating money and expanding to the outermost circles as fast as possible. This is not the case. The numbers are, to a large degree, irrelevant. By this I mean that people with large income-producing jobs frequently live in the innermost circle because they manage their money so poorly. On the other hand, people who manage their money efficiently and simply, frequently move through to the outermost circles, albeit, with fewer dollars.

So, the acquisition or loss of money is not what moves you from one circle to the next during your life. More money does not equal more power, more security, better health, instant retirement, or whatever you might be hoping for. And less money does not mean that you are doomed. It is the effective and efficient management of money that will make your goals attainable.

You have all read stories of little old ladies who die and leave million-dollar endowments to the local university. They are usually modest people who were prudent, consistent in their savings and investing habits, and moderate in their behaviors and desires. They frequently worked hard, improved their skills as needed, and never seemed to be following the crowd. At some point, they became mindful and found their way to the hub of the wheel. What propelled them to move there doesn't matter. What matters is that at some point, for some reason, they slowed down and began to connect with the consequences of their decisions. They became mindful of what they were doing.

Will simply working harder and longer do the trick? The answer is emphatically no. Most of the poor work extremely hard every day. They are not poor because they do not work. They are poor because they perform work that is little valued and is poorly paid; this work does not require a high level of skill. Skill and education are the assets that usually command higher salaries. These assets are often the insurance that keeps you afloat when economic times are tough. In the future, developed countries will need more and more skilled workers, particularly in technological services. You are already seeing jobs that call for unskilled labor being moved to developing countries. Where U.S. factory workers could once move to another local factory if they lost their jobs, the closest factories may now be in another state or another country. Being mindful of these facts, you should strive to become as skilled and/or educated as you can. Be mindful of the very real need to be a life-long learner.

And remember that your skills and your knowledge, everything you learn, is the only thing that you cannot lose. No one can steal what is in your head. Your television can be taken, along with your computer or your car; your house can burn down. But you cannot not know what you know. You can lose it through lack of use or because you become ill or die, but so long as you are a healthy, functioning human being, cultivating a love of learning will serve you well.

Finally, while you're taking time to breathe, pause and be aware of debt. Begin to be mindful of the difference between what can be said and what can be done. Advertisers urge you to get the good things in life, because you deserve it. But the way to get the good things is often to charge it. Advertising can target you and put pressure on you. You can succumb and indebt yourself. Or, you can get in touch with the reality of your dollars and make your decisions based on fact rather than on illusion.

REFLECT

Most people find themselves trapped in the center circle at some point in their lives. If that is your condition, the quality of your life can range from very hard to just getting by, no matter what your income level might be. Many people work long hours each week for low wages and find that there is not enough money for the basics. A minimum wage job, starting on June 24, 2008, will pay $6.55/hr. ($6.55 x 40 hrs = $262/ week) before taxes are withheld. This is hardly sufficient to rent a decent place to live and buy decent food and clothing here in the U.S. You find yourself checking out food banks and thrift stores. You rent apartments with several other people in order to make the rent. And you probably use public transportation because to purchase and maintain a vehicle is financially beyond you.

Subsisting at this stage usually means that the skills that you have are not financially valuable. This does not mean that the work you do is not valuable and necessary. Or, that you are not valuable. Some of the lowest paid jobs are critical to the day-to-day functioning of our society, and the people who perform them are valuable human beings. But the skills required to do this work usually are not difficult to come by and therefore, they are not financially valued.

Improving your skill level or combining your efforts with those of several other people are the only ways out of this fix. And that is a tall order, because most people who must devote their energy to making ends meet in this center circle, work so much that they have very little time to get extra training or education of any kind. Many people join the military to obtain a stable, structured living environment where in return for fighting many of their daily needs are met. These people can also take advantage of education programs and GI bill benefits. Some people become affiliated with local agencies that offer job training or skill improvement. Occasionally, an employer will pay for extra training on the job so that the employee will become more valuable to the employer in the future. This is usually a good deal for all concerned.

At the other extreme, let's say you make quite a bit of money but you still live in the inner circle. You are making money and spending every bit of it. There is no breathing room. If you are happy and you like your life, you're probably not reading this book. But if you are tired and wondering where all the money goes and how long you will have to work so hard, then mindfulness will offer you a pathway out. You must change your reality, little by little, until your life begins to make sense to you. Any time your life does not make sense to you, then it's probably not the life you really want.

Suppose you have educated yourself and you are making what you consider a decent living. Let's say you are single and make $50,000 annually at your job. What does this really mean?

Gross pay = $50,000 per year
18% income tax (estimate) = $8,925
3% state tax (estimate) = $1,500
7.65% Social Security/Medicare tax = $3,825

That $50,000 job just netted you: $35,750 a year. That is $2,979 a month or $1,490 twice a month.

Now, let's say you make $50,000 annually and you are self-employed.

18% income tax (estimate) = $8,925
3% state tax (estimate) = $1,500
15.3% Social Security/Medicare tax = $7,650

If you're self-employed, that $50,000 per year job really nets you only $31,925 a year, $2,660 per month or $1,330 twice a month.

As the average annual household income in the U.S. in 2006 was approximately $48,000, these numbers describe a great many people, whether they are single, coupled, or have children. Be mindful of these realities. If you make $50,000 annually, and you and your family were to try to live on $2,979 per month, there would scarcely be any money left to pay debts, whether that is a car payment, a college loan payment, or a free-floating credit card on which you've bought hundreds of little items you can no longer remember.

Here, the great impediment to progressing out of the inner circle is debt. If you improve your skills and education and manage to get higher paying work, you will begin to see a bit more money and you will think about buying things. But if you have already indebted yourself along the way, your debts may hold you back. When you make a debt in the present you are promising to give away the money you make in the future. Your debt can become a ball and chain you drag from decision to decision. Whether that happens or not depends on the reason you choose to indebt yourself. If you have taken on a reasonable amount of debt in order to enhance your education or training, you have a better chance of success. But if you have taken on debt in order to buy "stuff", you may find yourself financially trapped again, though looking at bigger numbers.

No matter what your income, it's important to take a close look at this center circle. The old adage is true: take care of the pennies and the dollars will take care of themselves. It is always wise to examine how you manage your basic expenditures.

Paying bills is rarely fun, but paying them promptly, regularly, and without a lot of difficulty is like greasing the wheels – everything runs more smoothly. You experience less stress. To the extent that you can arrange for your bills to be paid automatically, it may be to your advantage to do so, either by automatic draft, automatic debit, or some other method that is offered. But keep in mind that automatic payments take the place of sitting down and writing a check. They do not take the place of listing the checks in your check register or balancing your checkbook. In other words, even if you have your basic bills set up to be paid automatically, you must still keep track of that money.

Keep your organizational system simple. Most software offers much more accounting that what the average person actually needs. You can still keep good records with a pencil and a piece of paper. Or, you can check out some of the Internet money management systems that can update your information automatically so you don't spend any time inputting data. (Try www.mint.com for one.) Whatever organizational method you choose, make sure it is simple, not time-consuming, and provides you with the information you need. You are not organizing your money to be virtuous. You are organizing it so that your life will be easier and so that the time you have left in this life will be more pleasurable for you.

One of the most precious realizations that can come from being mindful is the awareness of death. I don't mean this is a morbid or depressing way. I mean this in terms of our ability as humans to wake up to the notion that our lives are finite. Do not think for a moment you will not die. Viewed from this perspective of reality, life becomes limited, and our day-to-day time begins to look much more like the precious commodity it is. Do you really want to spend your precious time arguing? Shopping? Running from here to there? Do you feel that you have so much time left in your life that you can afford to waste hours and days of it doing things you hate to do? The chaos brought about by uncontrolled finances will eat up your time. You may not realize that the chaos is a consequence that you, yourself, set into motion, but it is.

So back to mindfulness. To use mindfulness daily as a technique to stay connected to reality will insure that you make your financial decisions from a true, calm place, not from a place of fear or illusion. The subprime mortgage disaster and resulting foreclosures epitomize what can happen when people make their decisions from a place of illusion that is not connected to reality. Lenders loaned money despite the reality of the borrower's capability to repay, and borrowers borrowed money despite the reality of their inability to repay the debt when the interest rates changed. Everyone involved signed on to pretend together that it would all be okay. And then, when it all collapsed, everyone claimed to be completely shocked by the outcome. It was as though thousands of people had planted weeds and were flabbergasted to find that weeds came up.

So this little book is offering you a kindly dose of mindful reality. I am urging you to stay connected, to remain in the present, to practice mindfulness, and to handle your money accordingly. There are many web sites that will answer any question you have about simple money management. There are many books written on the subject where you can find an answer to any money question imaginable. This book is not trying to take the place of those resources. This book wants to get your attention. Money is not magic. It is a simple skill that anyone can master. Keeping yourself sufficiently protected and defended financially is as worthy of your attention as buying warm clothing to protect yourself against the cold. You would never plan to spend the winter in Alaska without warm clothing. But how are you protected financially? We know that in the future, laws will change, geopolitical crises will occur, economic cycles will run, and illness and injury will rear its head. You cannot know exactly what is in store. You must try to remain in the present and be mindful of what you are doing at all times. This will help you make sound, reality-based decisions that will add a measure of peace to your life.

CONSIDER

BUYING OR RENTING

You need a roof over your head. You either rent a place owned by someone else, or you buy a place with the help of a mortgage lender. Let's look at renting first. Many people believe that renting is throwing away money. It is not. Renting is keeping a roof over your head that you are not responsible for. The owner of the premises is responsible for the mortgage, the taxes, the insurance, the upkeep, and every little expense that arises. You are responsible for insuring your own stuff, (the contents of your place). Some people stop renting too soon. They feel compelled to buy. Only if you mindfully examine the expenses you would incur in each situation, will you make the right decision. Emotionally, you may be dying to own a house, but if it would be to your financial advantage to rent for one more year or five more years, you will be better off to stay calm and heed the numbers.

When you buy a house, you are responsible for its taxes, its maintenance, its landscaping, and any problems that arise. Owning a home can be a good thing, but owning a home that you cannot afford will make you want to run screaming out the front door. Be mindful about whether you decide to rent or to buy, and if you buy, buy a modestly priced house. Prior to the subprime collapse, chances were good that a lender would be willing to loan you more for a mortgage than you could reasonably afford. Just because the mortgage crisis has run its course, don't let down your guard. You must still take responsibility for your finances. Don't decide what monthly payment you can afford based on your gross salary. Figure it based on your monthly net salary – your take-home pay. See how much of your take-home pay you can comfortably send to the mortgage company and perhaps more importantly, see how comfortable you will be once your mortgage is paid, trying to live on the remaining money. Check in with yourself. Stop. Be mindful. If you're not comfortable, don't buy the house.

Lenders will point to the future. You will make more money down the line so this monthly payment will seem small five years from now. That may be true, or it may be false. Five years is a long time to suffer if you're hanging by a rope that you, yourself created.

Lenders will remind you of the tax benefits to owning a house. But this can be deceiving. At the moment, the interest paid on mortgages is deductible on schedule A of your federal income tax return, if you itemize. You are also allowed to take what the IRS calls a standard deduction. However, you are not allowed to take both. You may take either the standard deduction or the total of your schedule A deductions, whichever is higher. The standard deduction is raised nearly every year, and in many cases, this has made the standard deduction greater than the schedule A deduction, which includes the mortgage interest of modestly priced homes, rendering that mortgage interest useless as a tax benefit. In addition, the idea of eliminating the mortgage interest deduction entirely is batted around at just about every session of Congress, so even though it is available now, there is no guarantee that it will be available in the future.

And remember that buying a house costs more than you think. To buy a house, most people obtain a mortgage. The interest rate of that mortgage is important, because in most cases, you will be paying on that loan for many years. The interest rate, the amount you borrow, and the length of the loan (15 or 30 years), are used to calculate the monthly mortgage payment. But that only covers what is called, P & I, principal and interest, on the loan. To that monthly amount are added real estate taxes and homeowner's insurance. So, you must be mindful of all these costs when you are estimating your monthly payment.

If you do not have 20% of the purchase price of the house for a down payment on the loan, you will likely have to pay something called PMI (private mortgage insurance). This must also be calculated into your monthly payment and will increase it.

There will also be closing costs to finalize the loan. Closing costs are calculated based on the amount you are borrowing and the offer the lender is making. Shopping for lenders who give good deals is always smart. Remember, when you take out a loan, you are literally buying money. You don't want to pay more for it than you must.

Once you obtain your house, and your mortgage, it is wise to have your monthly mortgage payment automatically deducted from your checking account. Your payment will never be late and you can set the date of the draft so that it coincides with your payday. This method also saves you from worrying about it.

Once you have your mortgage, get a copy of the amortization statement from the lender. This is a long list that shows each payment and how much is applied to interest and to principal, and the running balance. It is a mathematical certainty that if you pay your regular monthly payment plus the principal amount due for the following month, you will pay your mortgage off in half the time. In other words, you will pay off a 30-year mortgage in 15 years. The amount of money you will save is staggering. For example, say you finance a $200,000 house for 30 years at 6.5%. Your monthly principal and interest payment would be $1,264. After 30 years, you would have paid $255,086 just in interest. If you could pay that same house off after 15 years, the amount you would have paid in interest would be only $113,600, a savings of $141,487.

And, if you are able to do so, do not forego paying your mortgage off entirely just because you don't want to miss the mortgage interest tax break. If you intend to stay in your house, pay it off. It may be your biggest asset and it is one you totally control. You decide whether to keep the house up or not, or maintain landscaping, or make repairs. There is no middle man, as with stocks, bonds, or cash. There is just you and your house. And no matter what the future may bring, if your house is paid off, you have a roof over your head that cannot be easily taken from you. This is a critical part of your financial security. Be very mindful of these facts as you make your decisions.

UTILITIES

Presumably, wherever you live, you will want electricity, heat, water, telephones, and so forth. So let's look at these expenses too. Your goal here is to keep your bills as unchanging as your mortgage payment. You always want to know the definite cost of your expenses, because you almost always know the definite amount of your paycheck.

Utility bills should be levelized. This means that instead of opening your bills each month and getting surprised by the amount, you know what the bill will be, within a dollar or so, because it is based on the previous 12-month average. This will not save you money. But it will make your monthly cash flow easier to manage because it will decrease the volatility. You might want a surprise for your birthday but you don't want it to come in the form of a bill. When it comes to managing your money, no surprises should be your mantra.

TELECOMMUNICATIONS

Telecommunications has become a huge expense for households. Here I include a telephone land line, cell phones, internet services, cable TV, pagers, satellite radio etc... Making decisions about these items actually takes quite a bit of time up front, and rigorous scrutiny of existing bills in order to see exactly what you are paying for. This is not easy. Telecommunication companies send out some of the most complicated invoices ever devised. It can be extremely difficult to try to understand which services you are receiving and how much you are paying for those services. But if you carefully sort them out, the effort will be well worth it. And don't forget: the goal here is not to reduce services you really want. It is to eliminate services that you don't want. Being mindful does not mean depriving yourself. It means knowing what you are paying for and what you are getting, and being sure that what you're getting is what you really want. When you review your bills, keep these thoughts in mind:

1. What am I paying for?
2. Do I want these services?
3. Can I get these services for less money?

Many people, when they actually take the time to review these bills, find that they are paying for services they don't want, and often, didn't even know they had. Eliminate what you do not want and reduce what you have too much of. Many people these days use their cell phones exclusively and do not pay for a land line. Don't keep a land line out of habit. Keep it out of need. If you do not use your land line and you use your cell phone 100% of the time, then stop paying for the land line. Of course, if you have dial-up Internet or DSL, you will have to keep your land line. Many people keep their land lines for emergencies. If you are using your land line only in emergencies, then reduce the cost of that line by eliminating the local and/ or long distance packages frequently attached to those lines. These packages are costly, especially when they are not being used. Regarding the internet, do consider high speed cable and be open to new technologies not yet invented. Competition and efficiency usually result in lower prices.

CABLE TELEVISION/INTERNET

With regard to cable TV, many people still use analog cable even though it costs nearly the same as basic digital cable. Analog provides the consumer with fewer channels than digital, plus the HD (high definition) takeover is soon to be upon you. Look into this. You might save money with digital cable or you might pay a bit more and get many more cable choices. Don't overlook satellite networks.

FOOD

Food is always a big expense, especially when you consider ALL the food in your budget – food that you prepare and food that you eat out. Again, consider the reality of your life. If you eat out often because of your schedule, then try to keep your expenses per meal to something reasonable that you can afford. If you enjoy cooking and eat home a lot, then be cognizant of what you are buying on your shopping trips. The one thing you do not want to do is to stock the house with groceries and eat out all the time. If you do that, you have just invested a big chunk of your money in food inventory. Your money is in your cupboards. Whether you cook at home or eat out has nothing to do with virtue. Just be realistic about your life. If you only have coffee in the morning, eat lunch out, and cook dinner at home, then you would probably not purchase breakfast or lunch food at the grocery store and stock it. Being mindful of your day-to-day activities, and being realistic and honest with yourself, will help you make smarter purchases.

GASOLINE/TRANSPORTATION

Gas is a big expense and will, no doubt, get to be a bigger one. The oil wars will be fought for quite awhile yet, and as new consumers arrive on the scene from developing nations, the demand for oil will continue to increase. As supply becomes further strained, the price of gas will continue to rise. A small, gas efficient vehicle may become a necessity. And, of necessity, you are going to have to become more mindful of your transportation dollars.

How much do you want to spend on transportation? Instead of going out and getting a vehicle and then figuring out if you can handle the payments, let's do this deal the other way around. Let's do it mindfully. How much do you want to spend to transport yourself from here to there? If you buy a new car, or lease a new car, and you have a $500/month car payment, plus you spend $160/month for gasoline, plus you spend $100/month for insurance, plus another $75/month for maintenance, plus $20/month for registration and licensing, that vehicle is costing you $855/month. That is over $10,000 a year for transportation. This is a category you should examine closely. Money can be saved. Cars can be sold. Insurance limits can be changed. Modestly priced vehicles (or used ones) can be purchased. In other words, cars are a big expense that can be reduced. Don't be afraid to sell a car, even if you take a loss. Under some circumstances, it is better to take the loss and get out from under the crazy car payment. No one wants to lose. But sometimes absorbing a loss on the front end can be a benefit to you in the long run. Hanging onto a bad deal because you don't want to realize the loss is often stupid. Sometimes it makes more sense to say, that was too bad and I lost money, and move on, trying to make better, more mindful decisions in the future. It is okay to make a mistake. You do not have to endure a bad decision forever. You do not have to punish yourself.

Remember this about vehicles: they depreciate. They become worth less over time, but they do not become worthless. Their fair market value decreases because they are machines and machines lose their value with use. But vehicles that run well, do not become worth less to you. Realize this distinction and be mindful of it. If you have a vehicle that is more than 10 years old but it runs reliably and gets you wherever you want to go, then it has intrinsic value to you, even when the book value (fair market value) may be next to nothing.

One final word on vehicles. If you are selecting your vehicle based on what you perceive to be your identity, then you are making a decision from a place of fear. If you are a kind and compassionate person, no one will care what you are driving. If you are a jerk, the car has not yet been built to convince others that you are wonderful. You are who you are and it has nothing to do with your vehicle. Find your true nature. It will be easier than finding a car that will tell you who you are.

INSURANCE

Once you have acquired these assets, it is prudent to purchase insurance to protect them. There are various types of insurance. Auto, home, life, medical, disability, and long-term care are the basics. Mindfulness plays a big role in insurance purchases. Do not allow yourself to be sold insurance. Go out and buy insurance. That is a very different thing. Become an informed insurance shopper. This is not difficult. You only need to know a few important things. I'll list them here and then explain each point more fully.

1. Never buy insurance from a place of fear.

2. Insure for big losses, not small losses. Insuring for small losses is too expensive. It is a bad financial deal.

3. Assume more of the risk by having high deductibles, not low ones. Low deductibles will cost you a lot of money that you will rarely get back. I am not suggesting that you want to assume insane amounts of risk. I am saying that it is not mindful to bet against yourself. Be realistic about your life.

4. Always put your insurance dollars into high liability limits with a reputable company, so that if you make a mistake, and someone else is hurt and their property is damaged, you have enough insurance to make the other person whole again, and they will not have to sue you personally to get the rest of their medical bills paid or their vehicle repaired.

5. If you have small children, buy term life insurance – as much of it as you think it will take to raise and educate your kids in the event of your premature death. If you don't have children, your need for life insurance just dropped a lot. You might still want to buy some, but it is no longer imperative.

If you filter all of your insurance decisions through these considerations, you will get the most bang for your insurance buck, get the best coverage, and protect yourself to the best of your ability. Do not rely on your insurance agent to make these decisions for you. The insurance agent's job is to provide you with the information you need and then sign you up. Good insurance agents do what they can to keep you protected and to keep your business. They check back with you to see if any life events have occurred that would necessitate a change in your insurance. But if you know what you want, then you don't have to rely on the agent having the time, inclination, or knowledge to help you make good decisions. You can make good decisions for yourself, and instruct the agent on what you want.

Most people buy insurance because they are frightened into it. They leave a visit with their agent convinced that catastrophes they hadn't even thought about are suddenly imminent, but confident that the papers they have just signed will protect them against all dire consequences. This is far from true.

Let's look at vehicle insurance. There are essentially two big parts to auto insurance: the liability part (someone else and their property are hurt or damaged as a result of something you did), AND the comprehensive/collision part (which involves damage to your auto). You want to make sure that you have high liability coverage because that is what the insurance company will have to pay if you make a mistake and someone else is hurt and their vehicle damaged. In other words, if you cause an accident and the total cost of medical bills and property damage is $150,000, but you have a liability limit of only $25,000, then the insurance company will pay the $25,000 and that's all. The remaining $125,000 is either left unpaid, it's paid personally by you, or the other person sues you to get the money because they still have medical bills to pay.

In the comprehensive/collision part of auto insurance, you are offered a deductible. A deductible is the amount of money you are willing to pay up front in the event of a claim. For example, if you have a $250 deductible, you are telling the insurance company that you are willing to assume the risk of paying for only the first $250 of repairs and no more than that. Because the insurance company has to assume everything over $250, it charges you a lot in premiums to keep that deductible so low. If you were to raise that deductible to $500 or $1,000, your premium payment would be greatly reduced because the insurance company does not have to assume as much risk.

Now, remember item number 2 above: insure for big losses, not small losses. It will cost you a lot of money to make sure that if you dent your bumper, you only have to pay the first $250 to repair it. In fact, over time, you may pay far more in premiums than what it would cost you if you dented your bumper and if you wanted to fix it and pay for the entire repair yourself. All these decisions are highly personal. You may be a careful driver, or maybe you drive drunk; rarely drive at night or only drive at night; drive 300 miles every day or hardly drive at all. Decisions on insurance are not one-size-fits-all. Stop and be mindful of the life you lead. Consider what will work best for you.

If you raise your comprehensive deductible to $1,000 and your car, worth $15,000 gets stolen, you will not mind writing the check for the first $1,000 in order to get yourself another car. Many people drop their comprehensive and collision coverage on old cars, because they are beyond theft and beyond repair. It is not that these cars could not be stolen or damaged, but that the chances of them being stolen are low, as are the chances that you would take great pains to repair them if they were damaged. Thus, you do not pay to keep coverage you will probably never use.

But never drive without liability insurance. Most states require this insurance because everyone makes mistakes, and others should not have to suffer because of your errors. You also don't want your mistakes to bring you to complete financial ruin if you can avoid it.

Discuss these ideas with your agent. It will not be the first time he or she has ever heard them. The agent will gladly raise your deductibles, or drop collision or comprehensive, and raise your liability coverage. In the end, you will have better protection, often for less money.

If you rent an apartment, it is wise to insure its contents. Renter's insurance does not cost very much, although it is expensive for what you get. Don't forget that again, you are protecting against the day you return from lunch to find that everything in your apartment has been stolen. You are not trying to insure against someone taking one television. So, you want to check on the deductible for the renter's insurance. You want a high deductible. You do not want to send away your premium dollars every month to the insurance company so that you only have to pay the first $250 in the event you have to replace something that costs $300. That is a waste of your money.

If you own a house, and you have a mortgage on it, you must have homeowner's insurance; the lender requires it. But again, remember, you want high liability limits and high deductibles. You are protecting yourself against the day you come home from the movies and your house is gone – swept away by a tornado or hurricane. You are not trying to protect against having to pay more than $250 if a window breaks. If you keep your deductible low ($250) you will pay hundreds of dollars to the insurance company so that if something minor occurs and you make a claim, you will only have to pay the first $250. Raise that deductible to $1,000 and keep the premium dollars in your pocket.

On the other hand, make sure that you have good liability limits. In other words, make sure there is plenty of money to cover the costs if someone is hurt at your home. Remember: high liability limits and high deductibles. It is the most efficient use of insurance dollars.

If you own a house and a car that are insured with the same company, and you have other assets you'd like to protect as well, you might want to purchase what is called an umbrella policy. This is a liability policy with high limits, usually a million-dollars, that kicks in when your car or homeowner's policy has hit its limits. It means that you have enough insurance to make someone whole again if they have suffered because of your error. It means that your assets are protected. It means that you are less likely to suffer financially if you are sued.

For people with small children, life insurance is a necessity. In the event that you leave this life before you are expecting to (and doesn't everyone?), the children will have to be raised, educated, and prepared to start their own adult lives. This duty may fall to the surviving spouse, or if both parents are gone, it may fall to a friend or relative who has been designated to raise the children. No matter who handles the job, it will be much easier if there is money available.

Young parents should buy as much term insurance as they find comfortable. In other words, if you are in your thirties and you have three children under the age of seven, you and your spouse might want to purchase $250,000 or $500,000, or $750,000 or even a million dollars worth of term insurance on each other. Be mindful here. Consider the age and health of the parents being insured, the number and ages of children involved, the overall health of the family, and so on. Do not buy out of fear. Buy out of prudence. And trust the actuaries. The reason term insurance is relatively cheap is that the likelihood of thirty-year-olds dying young is pretty slim. Some people do die young, of course, but in this country, most thirty-year-olds do not. So just be prudent and reasonable.

Once the children are grown, you may keep the insurance, if it suits your financial plans to do so, or you can cancel it. But if the kids are grown and gone, it has served its purpose. Don't keep insurance you no longer need.

If you don't have children, then buying life insurance is a choice. Be sure you have a reason for buying it. Many people purchase term insurance to complete a financial plan, to make sure a loved one will have enough money in the event of the insured's death, or to make money available upon one party's death to pay off some major debt, like a mortgage. Plain, relatively inexpensive term insurance will solve all these problems. Term insurance does not usually have any cash value. If you die while the policy is active, your beneficiary will get the face amount of the policy. If you stop paying on the policy and it lapses, your insurance simply stops.

Whole life insurance is the kind of insurance that will produce a cash value, eventually, years down the line. It is marketed as an investment insurance (a forced savings) and it is very expensive. Discuss this option at length with your agent before buying whole life. Make sure you are convinced that this would be a good use of your insurance dollars.

Medical (health) insurance is the brass ring these days. Fifty million citizens do not have health insurance in the U.S. There is much debate over how to insure more citizens, but no solutions have been established. Again, keep in mind that you want to insure for big losses, not little ones. If you do not have health insurance through your employer, and you are not yet 65 years old and entitled to Medicare, then you have very few options. One of your options, however, is to purchase a private policy of health insurance on the open market. Again, be mindful of the deductibles. If you try to purchase a type of policy that pays for every doctor visit and prescription drug, you will not be able to afford the policy. However, if you try to purchase a policy that will cover you in case you become seriously ill and land in the hospital for an extended period of time, and if you are willing to pay the doctor out of your pocket when you need an occasional office visit, you will find that reasonable policies, though scarce, are available.

In this situation you are looking for health insurance to cover catastrophic care. In other words, just like with homeowner's insurance, you are not trying to cover the small things, such as going to the doctor when you get a cold. You are trying to protect yourself against big losses, like a surgical procedure that will require a hospital stay. The amount you pay in premiums each month will reflect how much risk you are willing to assume. If you feel you must have a policy that pays for every doctor visit and every prescription, you could easily find yourself saddled with a policy that costs well over $500 per month. But if you maintain your health, take reasonably good care of yourself, and don't mind paying for the occasional check-up, you can purchase a more reasonably priced policy to protect you against large claims.

This is a difficult time in the U.S. for medical insurance and for medicine in general. The best way to protect yourself is to stay well. It is difficult to stay well and healthy without being mindful. Being mindful of your activities, your stresses, your food, your relationships – being mindful of your life in general – will prompt you to slow down, to pay attention, to assess your life and to make better decisions – decisions that will ultimately save you money.

Even with your best efforts, however, you may become too ill or too injured to work. At that point you would have to rely on others for help. Most people think first of Social Security Disability as a safety net for this occurrence. But while that net certainly does exist, the statistics on how long it takes to become approved for Social Security Disability benefits are not encouraging. As of this writing, those seeking disability benefits from the Social Security Administration frequently have up to a three-year wait. The process is full of appeals, which must be heard by Administrative Law Judges (ALJs), and there are simply not enough ALJs to hear all the cases. As a result, the backlog is tremendous. So, be prepared to wait, and be prepared to be without income while you wait. You will have to live off your own savings, or to rely on family or friends for help.

Also keep in mind that the definition of disability for social security purposes is stringent. The bar for qualifying is high, and the Social Security Administration denies benefits to many people who would seem quite disabled to you. The point is, Social Security disability insurance is not something to count on. You may get it, and you may get it quickly, but the chances are good that you will only get it after a prolonged struggle – if you get it at all.

In order to make the typical three-year wait a little less awful, you could purchase disability insurance. This is very expensive insurance, but sometimes it is offered in a benefit package through your employer, so it is always good to check there first to see if you have it or can sign on for it. If your employer offers disability insurance, that will probably be the cheapest place to get it. If not, then you're back to the open market and here again, there is not an abundance of products from which to choose. Here are a few things you should know about disability policies:

1. The insurance company can disagree with your doctor. In other words, your doctor may say you are disabled, but the insurance company can argue the point.

2. By law, benefits will be less than what you earn on your job.

3. Benefits are limited to a finite period of time, such as one, three, or five years.

4. Benefits have an elimination period – a number of days you are willing to be disabled and go unpaid before the benefits kick in. This could be 30 days, 60, 90, or even 120 days. The longer the elimination period, the cheaper the cost of the policy because you will have to use your own money to live during that time.

5. Policies frequently offer a cost-of-living rider, but you will have to pay extra for this. Without a cost of living rider, however, your money will not keep up with inflation and so it may be woefully inadequate in later years when and if you need it.

If you have to purchase a disability policy on the open market, then buy what you can afford. Anything will be helpful should you find yourself disabled. Again, the best way to avoid disability is to be mindful on the front end; mindfulness does not guarantee you won't become disabled, but the price of ignoring your health could be high.

One of the newest insurance products to come along in the last 20 years is long term care insurance. This is insurance to cover the cost of your care in old age. It was first thought that it would begin paying benefits when a person had to enter a nursing home. Some policies were later expanded to include in-home nursing care and some policies expanded further to include informal in-home care as well. But the deal you make for this kind of insurance is very, very long, and very, very expensive. You need this insurance if you have assets that you do not want to use for your own care. In other words, the people who buy this insurance tend to be well-off and have usually amassed a pool of investments and savings that they want to leave to the next generation. They do not want to use the money they have saved to pay for their care so they purchase long term care insurance to pay for their care in their old age. If you have accumulated assets that you do not want to spend, then you need to consider this insurance. The problem is that you may not need it for thirty or more years, or at all. It goes without saying that you have to be reasonably sure that the company you deal with will be around in thirty years. If you expect to reach the end of your life having accumulated few assets and little savings, there is very little reason for you to have this type of insurance.

If you do not have long term care insurance you must be prepared to use your money for your own care in old age. If you have not saved any money and your family cannot or will not care for you, or you need medical care beyond what family members can provide, then you must go to a nursing home that will accept payment from the government funded Medicare system. Medicare will pay a certain amount to a nursing home but the payments are not generous and your accommodations will be basic.

SAVINGS

I hope that one thing is clear by now. Saving money is not only a good thing, it is a critical step in taking care of yourself. But saving does not come naturally. You must be mindful about it. Always save . . . even if only five dollars a month. Always save. Save consistently. Save, no matter what. As you are learning to be mindful of all money decisions, be especially mindful of saving. Be mindful of why you are saving. Be mindful of how you are saving. This cannot be stressed enough. The old advice, – pay yourself first – is still as valid as it ever was.

Saving is math that works in your favor. Saving at a bank that pays interest on your savings account will allow you to receive compound interest. The idea of compound interest is not very interesting to people because they think it takes too long and because they don't see the beauty of the math. Compounding only becomes interesting to people when they begin to see what the math produces after about ten years of consistent savings. For the first ten years, the benefits don't look like much. But after ten years, the interest on your savings begins to explode. And it explodes in your favor.

Let's assume you do a one-time investment of $1,000 at an interest rate of 5%.

After 5 years, you have $1,276

After 10 years, you have $1,629

After 20 years, you have $2,653

After 25 years, you have $3,386

After 40 years, you have $7,040

Now, let's do the same example but let's change the interest rate to 10%.

After 5 years, you have $1,611.

After 10 years, you have $2,594.

After 20 years, you have $6,728.

After 25 years, you have $10,835.

After 40 years, you have $45,259.

You can see from this example what a tremendous affect an interest rate can have on money, whether you are earning it on an investment, or paying it on a loan.

Let's do one more example. The above examples are of one-time investments. In both you invested $1,000 and didn't add to it. Now, let's see what happens if you drop in $1,000 and save consistently over time. Let's say, $100 per month at 5%.

After 5 years, you have $8,084.

After 10 years, you have $17,175.

After 20 years, you have $43,816.

After 25 years, you have $63,032.

After 40 years, you have $159,960.

After investing $100 per month for 40 years, you have contributed $48,000. But the math of compound interest has more than tripled what you put in. Now let's change the interest rate to 10%.

After 5 years, you have $9,389.

After 10 years, you have $23,192.

After 20 years, you have $83,265.

After 25 years, you have $144,740.

After 40 years, you have $686,109.

Consistency, interest rates, and time can work wonders. There are many compound interest calculators online. Plug in the numbers that are appropriate for you and see what you get.

You might be surprised.

INVESTING

Saving money is not the same as investing money. You save with the goal of creating a nest egg that will help you during the difficult times, because, when you are mindful, and you slow down, you become more realistic; when you are realistic, you know that there will be difficult times. You invest with the goal of earning money from your money. There is a difference between accumulating money by saving, and earning money by investing.

But before going on to investing, let's take a look at your basics. Are you paying only for the services you want and use? Are you reasonably well insured and not overly insured out of fear? Have you reviewed your regular monthly bills to see that money is not being wasted? Have you noticed things you'd like to change and started the process of changing them, such as selling a car that is costing you too much? Are you focusing on being mindful in all areas of your lives so that you are slowing down, saying NO to things, valuing your time, and making genuine, long term changes?

There is no need to rush into investing. In fact, it would be inappropriate for you to begin to invest if your more immediate expenses are not being handled properly. It is not appropriate to invest in stocks if you cannot pay the water bill. It is not prudent to invest in bonds if you have no source of ready cash, like a savings account for a rainy day. If you don't have a safety net of savings, it is generally not a good idea to tie up your money in an investment, because if something arises and you need money, you either have to sell your investment (perhaps at a loss), or you have to indebt yourself to raise the money you need. In general terms, this is not an efficient way to handle your money.

But let's say that you have accomplished all of these tasks. You are happy with the life you've created and with how much it is costing you, and you are comfortable with your insurance coverages. You have a ready source of savings for emergencies and you still have money left over, so you are now ready to branch out to investing. What do you do? Investing usually comes in the form of stocks, bonds, cash, or real estate. You hope that by investing prudently and consistently, you will amass enough money to see you through to the end of your days, long after you are able to physically work and earn your own living.

Stocks are sometimes called equities and that term simply means ownership. Bonds are sometimes called debt, a term that indicates that money is owed. Cash is simply cash. Real estate is land or real property. The land can be developed or undeveloped. The real property can be residential housing or commercial space (offices, warehouses, etc.).

Here are the basics: You invest in cash through savings accounts that pay interest, through certificates of deposit (CDs) that pay interest, and through money market accounts that pay interest. CDs normally are for a set rate of interest and for a set period of time.

When you invest in bonds, you lend money to the company floating the bond. In other words, if you buy a General Electric bond for $10,000, General Electric is promising, in return for borrowing your $10,000, to pay you a certain amount of interest on that $10,000 for a specific period of time. At the end of that period, GE returns your $10,000 to you, having paid you the interest during the time you held the bond. It is an I.O.U.

When you invest in stocks, you buy a fraction of ownership in a company, usually called a share. In return for owning the stock of say, GE, you get a voting right. If the share price of GE stock goes up and you sell it, you have what is called a realized gain. If the share price of GE stock goes down from what it was when you bought it, and you sell it, you have a realized loss. When the share price fluctuates daily while you own the stock, you have an unrealized gain or loss depending on whether it goes up or down. You only realize a gain or loss at the time you sell the stock. Some stocks pay you dividends. Some do not.

With real estate, you make your money by owning real estate for rental purposes or by holding it while it appreciates in value and then selling it for a profit. If you decide to become a landlord or landlady, then you will be entitled to several tax deductions associated with owning these investments. Be sure to have your taxes prepared by a CPA so you don't miss any deductions.

These are the four basic concepts. All other investments flow from them. As complicated as investments may seem, and as complicated as they can get, these four concepts are at the foundation of all investments.

So, where do you go first?

Let's begin with cash. If you have $5,000 in a regular savings account and have amassed $5,000 more, you might want to begin by leaving $5,000 in the savings account in case you need it for emergencies, and put the other $5,000 into a money market account, which will earn you a higher rate of interest, or into a CD, which will also pay a higher rate of interest for a specific period of time. Both a money market account and a CD can be set up at a bank at no cost to you. Each bank will offer different rates and stipulate different lengths of time your money can be held so it's wise to call around to a few banks to see which one is giving the best deal. You can also check out rates online. This is an easy place to start and it is very safe.

If you feel ready to buy bonds, then you will want to check their ratings. Think of this as doing a credit check on a company to whom you are about to loan money. Bonds are rated by Moody's, and by Standard & Poors, and you will want to stick with highly rated bonds, those whose issuers are less likely to fail to pay you back (default). The ability of the borrower to pay back your money and all the interest promised is crucial. Poorly rated bonds are called junk bonds. You will see that junk bonds pay a high rate of interest. That is because of the extra risk you take in loaning them your money. There are many ratings between junk and high, so stick with highly rated bonds.

If you feel ready to buy stocks, then you will want to find a good stock broker who has been in the business during good times and bad. You will want to buy high-quality stocks from high-quality companies, representing a range of business sectors. You will want to remember to diversify by not buying too much of the same type of company. You will want to ask many questions and be able to reach your broker by phone or email whenever you reasonably need to.

Being mindful of your plans, remember this: if you find that you are dealing with a stock broker who cannot answer your questions in a way that makes sense to you, find yourself another stock broker, one who will make sure you are comfortable and have your questions answered. The intermediaries who sell you bonds and stocks are not fortune tellers. They do not know what is going to happen in the market place. No one does. They cannot accurately predict events. But they can be reasonably well educated about the market place, have a good strategy, be able to explain it, and stay consistent over time. If you do not find this in the first ten people you talk to, talk to eleven . . . talk to as many as you need to in order to find a good fit.

In order to be comfortable with real estate, you need to be prepared to deal with tenants, lenders, maintenance people, tax preparers, and you need to always put money away for the upkeep and repair of your property, in order to keep it valuable. If you have a mortgage associated with your rental property, then you must be prepared to meet the obligations of that mortgage, even when you are between tenants and have no rental income coming in. Being a landlord/lady, can be very rewarding, both personally and financially, but you need to be well aware of the risks before you venture into this investment product.

Being mindful of yourself, knowing yourself, is crucial when you are choosing your investment product. You should invest your money in things that interest you or that you know something about, that you will tend to keep up with, and generally, enjoy. For example, if you have no interest in stocks but love houses, consider buying residential real estate for rental. If you are very interested in buying and owning land, do that. If you love bonds but hate the stock market, stick with bonds. If you don't have a particular type of investment that you find interesting or enjoy, you will never care about it, and someone else will ultimately be making your investment decisions for you, which may be to your disadvantage.

Finding a trusted advisor is a critical first step. The search may be long but it will be well worth the effort. Interview many. They are not interviewing you. You are interviewing them. You are trying to decide whether you can trust this person, work with them, understand their thinking and their strategies, and in general, basically like them. Life is too short and there are too many professionals out there who want your business to be saddled with someone you don't really care for or who doesn't make you feel that your business and your concerns are important to them. You will pay them handsomely for their expertise and the best arrangement will be for you both to work together, so choose someone you like to work with.

Maybe that person is yourself. Technology now allows you to do a lot of your own investing online. You no longer need a broker at a brokerage house to place trades for you. You can trade online yourself, selecting your own investments based on your own research. This is attractive because it is inexpensive. On the other hand, you should probably ask yourself, whom would you rather rely on: someone who researches investments for a living (a broker or mutual fund manager) or someone who reads about them when they have spare time (you)? Of course, not all brokers are equal. As in any profession, some are quite superior and some are downright inadequate. You are looking for a superior broker/advisor. Be mindful of that, and don't be afraid to change if you are dissatisfied.

Many people have heard of mutual funds and invest in them, but don't actually understand what they are. Mutual fund companies own a family of funds. Each fund takes in the investment money of thousands of people. Each fund invests this large amount of money on behalf of its investors. Each mutual fund has it own investing goal. Some funds invest only in stocks, only in bonds, in combinations of stocks and bonds, or in only certain sectors of the economy such as utilities, industrials, or real estate. Some follow the well known indexes, like the S&P 500, and invest in the stocks listed on that index.

Each fund is managed by a fund manager or a group of managers. While you may not be familiar with the name of the fund, you may be familiar with the family name. For example, you have probably heard of Fidelity or Vanguard, Dreyfus or T. Row Price. These are fund family names. Each family may have many, many funds. Each fund may be managed by a different person. Not every manager and not every fund is successful, even if the fund family has a good reputation. In other words, to say that your investments are with Fidelity or Vanguard or Dreyfus, really says nothing about which funds you are in or whether or not your funds are making money. Every fund family has many funds, some of which are – and are not – successful. A fund is only as good as its manager.

Although trying to find a fund with a good track record and a good manager may feel like trying to find a needle in a haystack, the process has been made more efficient by a company called Morningstar. Morningstar reviews mutual funds and ranks them, using a five-star system. By using Morningstar, (which you can find on the Internet), you can narrow down the literally thousands of funds available to find what you're looking for, or you can investigate a fund that you think might interest you, to see if it does what you want your fund to do.

You can also go directly to the web site of the mutual fund company to check out the statistics on a particular fund and its goals to see if they match your own.

People frequently believe that if they are invested in mutual funds they are not invested in stocks or bonds. This is not true. The mutual fund you select usually will be invested in stocks, bonds, or cash or all three. The fact that your money is in a mutual fund only means that there is a middleman (a manager) between you and the ultimate investment (the stock, the bond). Because mutual funds take in so much money from so many people, however, you do get a kind of automatic diversification from mutual funds. For example, if you have $10,000 and you call your broker and buy 300 shares of XYZ stock, that is the only stock you own. If you take the same $10,000 and put it in a mutual fund that buys 100 stocks, then you will own a piece of each of those 100 stocks, so if one stock goes down, it will not affect you as much as if XYZ goes down. This is not to say that buying shares of a mutual fund is better than directly buying shares of a stock. It is saying that these investment vehicles are two different things. Be sure you understand the pros and cons of each before you make a final decision.

People who are not mindful, make their investment decisions without any awareness and as quickly as they can because it makes them uncomfortable to have to deal with finances. If this describes you, now is an excellent time to slow down, to think about your values, your hopes for the future, which investments interest you, and so forth, rather than to jump in, sign papers, and forget about it. You might panic and buy something because you think it's hot, or sell something because you think it's down which is, incidentally, the worst time to sell. There is no room for greed or panic in prudent investing. There is a real need for mindfulness, calm and patience, and above all, consistency.

RETIREMENT

You have probably heard a lot of talk about IRAs (Individual Retirement Accounts). There are basically two types: the traditional IRA and the Roth IRA. The traditional IRA is not as popular as it once was. It allows an individual to set aside money each year (the limits change with the laws) and to deduct that amount of money (with certain limitations) from the taxable income on his or her current income tax return, thereby paying less in taxes in the current year. Earnings on your IRA account are tax deferred, which means that you don't pay tax on them until after you've retired and begin to take the money out.

The Roth IRA is a bit different. You are still entitled to set aside a certain amount of money each year, but you cannot deduct it from your taxable income or report that deduction on your current income tax return. However, the earnings from that Roth IRA grow tax free. Not tax deferred. Tax free. The limitations on how much you can contribute to a Roth IRA change annually with the law.

The idea of IRAs is a very important one. In different ways, both reduce your taxes, but the concept of reducing your taxes is one to contemplate. You do not want to make your decisions by letting the tax tail wag the dog; that is not wise. The surest way to pay no tax is to make no money. But how many of you would prefer to live with no money rather than to pay taxes? You do want, however, to consider taxes in your financial decisions, because taxes will eat up your money. Any investment that you can make that is tax free, tax deferred, or pre-tax, is an opportunity. Sheltering your money from taxes allows you to keep more of your money, so you always want to look into products that do that.

A common one that is offered to many employees these days is the 401(k) retirement plan.

In the past, companies bore the burden of funding an employee's pension. But the days of company-paid gold watches and pensions after many years of service are over.

Fewer and fewer companies will be offering pensions in the future. The new method, in the form of a 401(k) plan , places the burden of funding retirement on the employee. When companies offered pensions, the company was responsible for making sure that you got your monthly pension check once you retired. With the 401(k) plan, the company is, in large part, not responsible. You are responsible for funding your retirement and for deciding how your retirement contributions are invested. If you choose to fund your 401(k) and you choose your investments wisely, then you may end up with a suitable amount of money upon retirement. If you choose to fund it minimally or not at all, and choose investments that don't do so well, your retirement will be much less successful – if you ever get to retire at all.

If your company offers a 401(k), you should participate in it because it is funded by pre-tax dollars and its earnings are sheltered from current taxes. But please pay attention to it. Pay attention to your choices. Seek help on this from professionals. The decisions you make – or maybe worse, fail to make – could affect you drastically down the line. What can you invest 401(k)s in? Nearly anything you choose, from a wide variety of funds. You can invest in stocks, bonds, or cash through your 401(k), or any combination of them. Seek professional guidance but remember that ultimately, these decisions are yours alone.

Along with the 401(k) a company may offer what is called a cafeteria plan. This is not a retirement plan but it is a pre-tax plan. It allows you to shelter money in a fund during the year to pay for certain specific items like medical bills and childcare. The important thing to remember when taking advantage of a cafeteria plan is that all the money you've contributed during the year must be used up to pay those bills by the end of the year, or you lose the money. You cannot withdraw any left over money if you do not use it for the specified purposes.

Try not to think of Social Security as the center of your retirement planning. It will be here for awhile, and if you have worked, you have paid dearly into it. But, as a society, we are moving toward a reduction in entitlements on every front. The trend is toward increasing self-reliance in an increasingly worldwide free market. This is not necessarily bad, but it is different from how your grandparents and parents lived and how they planned for their financial futures. As a result, being mindful becomes more important every day. Social Security/Medicare currently take 15.3% out of every paycheck in the country, up to the current limit, which, as of this writing, is $97,500 per year. If you are an employee, your employer pays half of that 15.3% and you pay the other half. If you work for yourself, you pay the whole 15.3%. This tax comes off the top of your income before you pay any income tax to the federal government or any income tax to your state government, or local taxes to your county or city, or sales taxes on purchases, or personal property taxes or real estate taxes or an assortment of other taxes.

So, let's be mindful once again. Let's use the example from earlier, when you saw that if you make $50,000 at your job, your real take-home pay was just $35,750 annually, or $2,979 per month (and if you are self-employed your net is even lower).

Remember that the average annual household income in the U.S. in 2006 was approximately $48,000 so these numbers may not be very far from what your actual paycheck may be.

Let's use your real take-home pay numbers to calculate where you want to live, what you want to drive, how you want to eat, how many methods you need to telecommunicate, and how much stuff you can't live without. Let's also use them to plan your savings, retirement, vacations, insurances, and education. Let's use the real numbers as you plan almost everything.

BE VIGILANT

What you will inevitably find if you use real numbers is that you cannot afford most of the things the government/business/advertisers say you can afford. There are simply not enough dollars to go around. You must prioritize. Many people have augmented their incomes by shopping with credit (unsecured credit on a variety of credit cards for which they pay unbelievably high rates of interest for the privilege of borrowing small amounts of money, often for long periods of time). Almost everyone does this, hanging on for dear life as the wheel spins faster and faster. This is one way you are asked to define success. You are invited to tacitly agree to ignore the real numbers and just keep earning and spending and indebting yourself. But if you buy into this line of thought, you remove yourself deliberately from reality and from being mindful. You will be shocked – shocked – when things do not work out for you. You plant weeds and are astonished when weeds come up.

I have asked you in this book to redefine success. Redefine it for yourself, personally. You should produce a definition that fits only you. It doesn't matter what that is. What matters is that you have slowed down long enough to acknowledge the reality of your life. You have become mindful of the truth of your life. You are beginning to see how much your creation is costing you in money, but also in time, which is much more precious. You are seeing that your decisions, even the smallest ones, impact your life.

I am asking you to rest in the calm center. I am asking you to change your mind.

It will change your life.